ALTERNATOR
BOOKS™

Law enforcement
ROBOTS

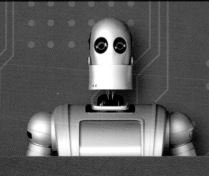

MARY LINDEEN

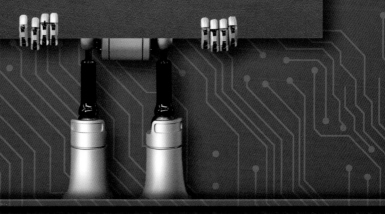

Lerner Publications ◆ Minneapolis

For Benjamin, expert technical consultant

Lerner Publications Company
A division of Lerner Publishing Group, Inc.
241 First Avenue North
Minneapolis, MN 55401 USA

For reading levels and more information, look up this title at www.lernerbooks.com.

Library of Congress Cataloging-in-Publication Data

Names: Lindeen, Mary, author.
Title: Law enforcement robots / Mary Lindeen.
Description: Minneapolis : Lerner Publications, [2017] | Series: Cutting-edge robotics | Audience: Ages 8–12. | Audience: Grades 4 to 6. | Includes bibliographical references and index.
Identifiers: LCCN 2016048096 (print) | LCCN 2016050337 (ebook) | ISBN 9781512440119 (lb : alk. paper) | ISBN 9781512449358 (eb pdf)
Subjects: LCSH: Law enforcement—Technology—Juvenile literature. | Robotics—Juvenile literature.
Classification: LCC HV7922 .L56 2017 (print) | LCC HV7922 (ebook) | DDC 629.8/92—dc23

LC record available at https://lccn.loc.gov/2016048096

Manufactured in the United States of America
1-42273-26130-2/21/2017

CONTENTS

LOST IN THE WOODS

In 2014 a Canadian family went hiking in the woods. They got lost and couldn't find their way out of the forest, so they used their cell phone to call for help. Local police sent out a search team with a tracking dog, but the dog couldn't find the family's scent.

Then the Royal Canadian Mounted Police brought in a drone with a camera on it. The drone flew over the forest and found the family. Information from the drone told rescuers exactly where the family was, and the police were able to go to the family and guide them out of the woods. Because of a robot, the family was safe.

A law enforcement worker flies a search-and-rescue drone in 2014.

CHAPTER 1

DEVELOPING LAW ENFORCEMENT ROBOTS

Drones are just one kind of robot that law enforcement officers use. Robots of all kinds are becoming common in police departments around the world. They can do jobs that are difficult, dangerous, or even impossible for humans to do, such as moving through collapsed buildings or taking apart bombs.

A drone known as the Guardian was designed by a Lebanese architect to find and save people drowning in the sea.

The idea of using machines instead of people to complete dangerous tasks began in the military. During World War II (1939–1945), the German army used remote-controlled mini tanks and flying bombs loaded with explosives. More recently, drones and robots were used to search caves and take **aerial** pictures during battles in Iraq and Afghanistan.

US Navy men look at a German remote-controlled robot known as Goliath in 1944.

FACTOID!

Law enforcement officers include police officers, sheriffs' deputies, state troopers, and public park police. Emergency medical professionals, firefighters, and rescue teams are not considered members of law enforcement.

DISASTER DUTY

On September 11, 2001, terrorists destroyed two skyscrapers at the World Trade Center in New York City. Thousands of people died. Debris from the fallen towers was piled high, and the spaces in the rubble were too small and dangerous for people or even rescue dogs to get through. Small robots called PackBots were brought in to help.

This robot, known as a Small Unmanned Ground Vehicle (SUGV), is similar to the PackBots used on September 11. The SUGVs have been used for military operations.

FACTOID!

Computers and the Internet are also part of our daily lives thanks to the military. The armed forces have supported the research that has led to new technology, including robots, computers, and the Internet.

PackBots move on wheels with heavy tread, so they can go where law enforcement agents and rescuers can't. PackBots took pictures from inside the debris piles in New York City to help rescuers decide whether they should dig into the rubble to search for people. It was the first time robots had been used to help in a disaster. A newer version of the PackBot was used in 2011 in Japan after a **tsunami** hit.

An updated PackBot was demonstrated at a technology company in 2011.

LAND AND SEA

Over the years, new robots have been put to use in many different ways by law enforcement. In 2013 the city of Kinshasa in the Democratic Republic of the Congo, a country in Africa, began using huge solar-powered robots to direct traffic. These tall robocops have red and green traffic lights as well as messages to tell people when it is safe to cross the road. They also have cameras to record traffic. Since the robots were installed, the roads in Kinshasa have become safer.

A robot directs traffic at a busy intersection in Kinshasa.

In 2015 **refugees** from Africa and the Middle East sailed to Europe to escape the violence in their home countries. Many of their boats ran out of fuel or began sinking at sea, and thousands of people drowned. So the Coast Guard in Greece began using robotic life preservers. These devices moved like Jet Skis to those struggling in the water. Up to five people could hold onto the preserver. Then the operators pulled the people to safety using a long rope attached to the preservers. This was the first time these robots had been used in a large rescue operation.

FACTOID!

Roboticists Without Borders (RWB) is a group of volunteer robotics experts who loan robots to rescuers and law enforcement groups around the world. Some law enforcement agencies can't afford to have the robots they might want or need, so RWB robots are loaned out for free to help in disasters.

CHAPTER 2

ROBOTS ON THE JOB

Robots are made differently depending on the jobs they are built to do. For instance, snakebots are built to slither on the ground like a snake. These robots can go over rough ground or into small places. Snakebots may someday slide through rubble to search for earthquake victims. Or they might slither through pipes to record criminal activity.

A snakebot imitates the movement of sidewinder snakes on sandy slopes.

FACTOID!

Underwater drones and underwater vehicles are some of the newest law enforcement robots. Along with cameras and **sensors**, these robots use **sonar** to operate and navigate in the water.

An underwater drone on display at a 2017 electronics show

One common job law enforcement robots have is to move or **disable** bombs. A human bomb expert uses remote controls to operate this kind of robot from a safe distance. The robot has cameras on it so the expert can see what the bomb looks like. The robot also has robotic arms and grippers on it, which allow the robot to handle the bomb. The operator can make the robot move the bomb to a safer place to destroy the bomb or disable it to prevent an explosion.

MERCY AND MIGHT

Search-and-rescue (SAR) robots are designed to move in dangerous or tight spaces. They have sensors, cameras, and GPS (Global Positioning System). These robots can detect dangerous chemicals and help operators to see into collapsed buildings and figure out whether there are people trapped inside. The robots also have attachments to pull people to safety.

This surveillance drone carries a camera and a life buoy. It flies over a beach in France in 2016 to demonstrate a rescue operation.

Other law enforcement robots are very strong. Some have heavy-duty jaws or gripping devices to tear through walls, cut metal, or rip open doors. Battering ram robots knock down walls or doors and break through windows. This allows law enforcement agents to safely deliver food, phones, or medicine in a tense **hostage** situation.

A team of police officers holds up bulletproof shields to show that these shields provide less protection than the robotic shield on the right.

WATCH IT!

Many robot features are designed for watching and reporting. Law enforcement officers use the cameras and sensors on drones and other robots to see and hear what's going on in places that might be too difficult or dangerous to enter.

Drones fly over an area to gather information. Other robots can be thrown over walls or into buildings to collect information. Still others have long, flexible arms. The arms allow robots to look under cars or in other places that are dangerous for humans to check out. Some are so small that people don't even know they're being watched when a robot is on the job.

FACTOID!

Some law enforcement robots are being used to control lawbreaking robots. Police in Japan use drones with nets to capture drones that are flying in restricted areas.

CHAPTER 3

CREATING a ROBOT

Police in Cleveland, Ohio, asked high school students to help build a bomb-detecting robot in 2016. The police wanted a robot that could quickly check suspicious packages at a political convention. The students built Scoutbot, a six-wheeled robot with a camera and night vision. They used a 3-D printer to make some of the parts. To make this robot, the students had to know about many different subjects, from chemistry to mechanical engineering. They also used math, computer coding, and communications technology. This knowledge is important for making any kind of robot.

BOT THOUGHTS

Since robots can be operated from a distance using remote controls, police robots could make it possible for officers who've been injured on the job to keep on working. These officers could do their work from a police station, using remotes or computers to direct robots on the street to write tickets, stop crimes, and help people in need.

Students display the robot they designed for use by Cleveland police in 2016.

WORKING WITH ROBOTS

Police robots are controlled by humans using cables, remote controls, or computers. Operators need to see what the robot sees and make decisions about where the robot should go. Then the robot operators can decide how the robot should approach a situation. Robot operators may also need to communicate with people through the robot. They may need to ask if anyone is hurt or tell people to move to a safer place.

All of these functions rely on computer software and electrical circuits. Those who build the robots must understand electronics and be able to code the robot correctly to respond to its operator. These robots need to be able to respond quickly and accurately in tense situations.

A robot inspects a power station in China in 2016.

FACTOID!

Computer scientists are working on creating swarmbots. These are small robots that can team up and work together. The idea came from watching ants work together. Swarmbots can be used to quickly map an area. Someday they might be used to search for and rescue people.

Swarmbots

ROBOTS IN ACTION

Robots must be able to respond to their operators, and they must also move and work well in many different situations. Engineers design and build complex machines. They experiment with robots to see which parts will make a robot more stable and reliable. Robots that walk on two legs fall over very easily, so most police robots roll on wheels or tracks. This helps the robots stay upright as they travel over uneven ground and in awkward spaces.

The sturdy wheels on this robot will help it to move easily over rough terrain.

FACTOID!

Some robots look as if they have eyes, even though they don't really need them. Scientists discovered that people sometimes think robots without eyes don't care about them. Robots with eyes seem friendly and helpful.

A robot's mechanical hands and arms are also very important. A robot that is working to disable a bomb may need to hold small objects and must work carefully and quickly. So the scientists creating the robot study how human fingers move. Then they can copy this motion in a mechanical hand.

ROBOT PSYCHOLOGY

It may seem surprising that scientists who study the mind and human behavior would work with robots. But it's important to know how people will react to law enforcement robots. For instance, psychologists want to know if kids would be more willing to talk to a small, friendly robot than a police officer. The science of law enforcement robots is the science of helping people.

CHAPTER 4

THE FUTURE OF LAW ENFORCEMENT ROBOTS

Many people believe police robots will make the future safer. Using police robots will help keep human officers out of danger. Robots may be able to respond to threats or rescue people more quickly and safely than human officers can.

A remote-controlled law enforcement robot shows how it would destroy a dangerous object during a demonstration in Germany in 2016.

But others worry that law enforcement robots will make the future less safe. Police robots carry many powerful tools and sensors, and they may be stronger than human officers. They can easily spy on people. Some people are concerned that robots will not be able to respond sensitively in tense situations, as humans can. They think that robots will scare people instead of helping them.

Police officers and children participate in the twentieth annual Cops for Kids Program in New Mexico. Some people are concerned robots will not be as helpful as human officers.

BOT THOUGHTS

Robots are machines. They can break down or stop working. They don't have **judgment**. They can't change their minds or make their own decisions. Some people think this means robots are dangerous. They aren't sure if robots should continue to be used. No one knows for sure how robots will be used in the future. Maybe someday you will help make these decisions about law enforcement robots.

Robots can also be **hacked**, reprogrammed, or stolen. New laws will have to be made to make sure people don't **interfere** with law enforcement robots. Laws will also have to be written that explain when and how law enforcement officers are allowed to use robots.

JUST THE BEGINNING

Scientists build new robots all the time. And police departments are just beginning to understand what robots can do and how they can be used to keep people, places, and property safe. The future will likely have many more law enforcement robots in it. Someday soon there might even be robots patrolling in your neighborhood. If you need help, you'll just ask the nearest robot!

A firefighting robot sprays water at a fire during a demonstration in China in 2015.

BOT PROJECT

The Robocops used in Kinshasa are able to turn around to direct traffic. With just a few simple supplies, you can make your own mini robot and learn one way to make a robot spin.

WHAT YOU NEED

- ⚙ wire cutters and pliers
- ⚙ 16-gauge copper wire
- ⚙ 1 AA battery
- ⚙ 3 neodymium disc magnets measuring
  ½ × ⅛ inches (1.3 × 0.3 centimeters)
- ⚙ red and green ribbon or yarn
- ⚙ scissors

WHAT YOU DO

1. Cut a piece of wire about 12 inches (30 cm) long. Bend it into a rectangular shape, with the two ends slightly overlapping in the middle of one of the long sides of the rectangle.

2. Wrap the loose ends of the wire around your finger so they make a circle. Make sure the circle is big enough to fit around the AA battery. Bend a small V shape in the middle of the opposite side of the rectangle.

3. Stack the three neodymium magnets on a counter, table, or other stable surface. Put the AA battery on top of the magnets, with the negative side down.

4. Put the wire over the battery. The bottom tip of the V shape should be resting on the tip of the positive end of the battery. The round shape at the bottom of the wire should be low enough to fit loosely around the magnets.

5. Let go of the wire. If it's placed properly, the wire will begin to spin around. If it doesn't, make adjustments as needed.

6. Tie a small red ribbon or string to one side of the wire. Tie a small green ribbon or string to the other side of the wire. Then you've got a tiny traffic cop robot working as fast as it can to keep traffic moving!

Note: This project should be done with adult supervision. The battery may get hot while the robot is running. If this happens, take the robot apart to let it cool down.

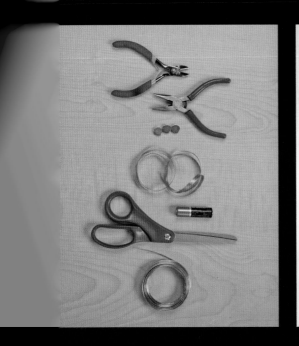

TIMELINE

1940s   Germany uses remote-controlled mini tanks and remote-controlled flying bombs during World War II.

1959–1975   The US military uses remote-controlled drones for reconnaissance during the Vietnam War.

1991   During the Gulf War, the US military has at least one unmanned aerial vehicle in the air at all times.

2001   PackBot robots are used for the first time following the collapse of the World Trade Center towers.

2011   Packbots are used at the Fukushima nuclear power plant after it is destroyed by a tsunami in Japan.

2013   Large robots designed to help direct traffic are installed in Kinshasa, in the Democratic Republic of the Congo in Africa.

2016   The Coast Guard in Greece uses robot life preservers to save drowning refugees at sea.

    China creates Anbot, the world's first armed police robot, which can deliver an electrical shock to subdue a suspect.

GLOSSARY

aerial: happening in the air

disable: to cause something to be unable to work in the normal way

hacked: changed or modified without permission

hostage: someone taken and held prisoner as a way of demanding money or other conditions

interfere: to prevent a process or activity from being carried out properly

judgment: the ability to come to sensible conclusions

refugees: people forced to leave their homes because of war, persecution, or a natural disaster

sensors: instruments that can detect changes in heat, sound, pressure, and more and send that information to a controlling device

sonar: a device used for finding things underwater by using sound waves

tsunami: a very large, destructive wave caused by an underwater earthquake or volcano

FURTHER INFORMATION

All about Robots
http://www.kidsdiscover.com/teacherresources/all-about-robots

Christensen, Victoria G. *How Sensors Work*. Minneapolis: Lerner Publications, 2017.

Cool Jobs: Wide World of Robots
https://www.sciencenewsforstudents.org/article/cool-jobs-wide-world -robots

Faust, Daniel R. *Military and Police Robots*. New York: PowerKids, 2016.

La Bella, Laura. *Drones and Law Enforcement*. New York: Rosen, 2017.

Law Enforcement Robots
http://www.learnaboutrobots.com/lawEnforcement.htm

Robocops Hit the Streets
http://magazines.scholastic.com/news/2015/04/Robocops-Hit-the-Streets

Spilsbury, Richard, and Louise Spilsbury. *Robots in Law Enforcement*. New York: Gareth Stevens, 2016.

INDEX

PHOTO ACKNOWLEDGMENTS

The images in this book are used with the permission of: background: © iStockphoto.com/chekat; design elements: © iStockphoto.com/Kirillm; © iStockphoto.com/Ensup; © 3alexd/iStock/Thinkstock; © iStockphoto.com/Ociacia; kirill_makarov/Shutterstock.com; © iStockphoto.com/leoblanchette; content: AP Photo/The Canadian Press/Jonathan Hayward, p. 5; © Ratib Al Safadi/Anadolu Agency/Getty Images, p. 6; © US Navy/Interim Archives/Getty Images, p. 7; © Scott Eells/Bloomberg/Getty Images, p. 8; © James Leynse/Corbis/Getty Images, p. 9; © Junior D. Kannah/AFP/Getty Images, p. 10; AP Photo/Carnegie Mellon University/Rex Features, p. 12; ZUMA Press, Inc/Alamy Stock Photo, pp. 13, 25; © GEORGES GOBET/AFP/Getty Images, p. 15; AP Photo/Robert F. Bukaty, p. 16; RICK WILKING/REUTERS/Newscom, p. 19; © VCG/Getty Images, pp. 20, 27; © Wendy Maeda/The Boston Globe/Getty Images, p. 21; © DIETER NAGL/AFP/Getty Images, p. 22; AP Photo/Wolfgang Kumm/picture-alliance/dpa, p. 24; © Giliane Mansfeldt/Independent Picture Service, p. 29.

Cover: © Jaromir Chalabala/Shutterstock.com (main); design elements: © iStockphoto.com/Kirillm; © iStockphoto.com/chekat; © iStockphoto.com/da-vooda; © iStockphoto.com/Ensup; © iStockphoto.com/eduardrobert.